HOW HIS BRIDE CAME TO ABRAHAM

Karen Sunde

BROADWAY PLAY PUBLISHING INC
New York
www.broadwayplaypublishing.com
info@broadwayplaypublishing.com

HOW HIS BRIDE CAME TO ABRAHAM
© Copyright 2006 by Karen Sunde

Cover photo by Robert N Redmond
First printing: February 2006

I S B N: 978-0-88145-304-1

Book design: Marie Donovan
Word processing: Microsoft Word
Typographic controls: Ventura Publisher
Typeface: Palatino
Printed and bound in the U S A

A slightly different version of HOW HIS BRIDE CAME TO ABRAHAM was published by Broadway Play Publishing Inc in June 2001 in the collection *Plays By Karen Sunde.*

HOW HIS BRIDE CAME TO ABRAHAM was first produced at Playwrights Theater of New Jersey (John Pietrowski, Producing Director), in May 2002.

ABE	Tzahi Moskovitz
SABRA	Lana Yemaya Nasser
GRAMMA	Marilyn Bernard
Voice-over of DOG-STAR	O T Carson
Director	Ken Marini
Fight direction	Rick Sordelet

HOW HIS BRIDE CAME TO ABRAHAM was subsequently produced by Praxis Theater Project, New York (Matt Bray, Producer) opening in March 2003.

ABE	Amir Babayoff
SABRA	Maya Serhan
Voice of GRAMMA	Emily Mitchell
Voice of DOG-STAR	Joe Saraceno
Director	Courtney Patrick Mitchell
Fight direction	Ian Marshall

HOW HIS BRIDE CAME TO ABRAHAM premiered at
The Unicorn Theater, Kansas City, MO. The cast and
creative contributors were:

ABE .... Michael Stock
SABRA .... Alyssa Cartwright
Voice of GRAMMA .... Merle Moores
Voice of DOG-STAR .... Joel Brady

Director ....Cynthia Levin

CHARACTERS & SETTING

ABE, *young soldier, by nature tender, bright, coarsened by grueling duty.*

SABRA, *young woman, ferocious, fine. Child's heart, locked in horrors*

Voices:

GRAMMA, ABE's *grandmother. Salty, warm as sunset, wise as time*

DOG-STAR, ABE's *platoon-mate—rough, officious, human. Also plays Ben, ABE's friend—exuberant, careless*

The action happens on (and in) a hill in South Lebanon. It feels like the news, but also requires magic.

An actual hill is not essential. An imaginative hill on a bare stage can also serve, as stage directions describe. Sound, light, music, and actors create this world. Trees and roots can be suggested by a few ropes hanging.

(Pre-Set: afternoon sun, bird sounds—music is light, like a dream. Offstage, soldiers moving on a gravel road. As lights go to black we hear soldiers; may be voice-overs—)

BEN: *(Off)* Look, I see one.

ABE: *(Off)* Keep moving, Benny.

BEN: *(Off)* It's a yellow bill! I win!

ABE: *(Off)* You don't see a yellow bill.

BEN: *(Off)* Just look, right there!

ABE: *(Off)* All right, but we shouldn't be...

BEN: *(Off, bumped off balance)* Auuh.

ABE: *(Off)* Watch out...

(Explosion offstage. House and stage black. Shouts—)

ABE: *(Off, terrified)* Benny!

DOG-STAR: *(Off)* God. Oh, God!

ABE: *(Off)* Help him!

DOG-STAR: *(Off)* Stop the blood.

(Flickering glow from explosion's fire)

ABE: *(Off)* Move him out!!

DOG-STAR: *(Off)* Abe's hit too.

ABE: *(Off)* Leave me. I'm all right. Go!

DOG-STAR: *(Off)* Go!!

(Dimly, lights up on ABE, sprawled in downstage corner, one foot bare, badly wounded).

ABE: *(As shock takes him)* Take it easy with Benny. Move! *(Desperate chant)* The Lord is my shepherd... The Lord is my shepherd... Oh God, why...?

(As tramping recedes; birds, insects, ABE *passing out, a soothing voice quickly corrects—)*

GRAMMA: *(V O)* The Lord is my shepherd, I shall not want. He maketh me to lie down in green pastures, he leadeth me beside the still waters, he restoreth my soul.

ABE: *(Near delirium)* Yeah that's it; Gramma, thanks for the thought, but give it to Benny.

GRAMMA: *(V O)* Yea, though I walk through the valley of the shadow of death...

ABE: God, Benny, why'd you have to stop here?

*(*GRAMMA *softly hums an Israeli folk song, as shock overcomes* ABE...)*

*(*ABE *is a very young Israeli Defense Forces [I D F] 2nd Lieutenant, breathing hard from pain, shock, and to keep himself from crying. He's frightened; his best friend has just been exploded, but he will handle himself like the man he has to be as long as he retains consciousness)*

(At sudden crackle from ABE's *field radio, he snaps awake. It could be, in fact, that the only "real" moments in the play are those when* ABE *hears the radio, and all else is the dream into which he escapes.)*

RADIO: *(V O)* Dog-star to Apex. Dog-star to Apex.

ABE: *(Dizzily)* ...What.

RADIO: *(V O)* Radio check.

ABE: *(Jerking awake)* Yeah. Yeah. You hear me?

RADIO: *(V O)* You're coming in clear.

ABE: *(Not wanting to know)* How's...Benny?

RADIO: *(V O)* He passed out. Just lost consciousness.

ABE: Get him the hell out of here!

RADIO: *(V O)* We'll send a squad for you.

ABE: Hell with me.

RADIO: *(V O)* You've gotta be in shock, Apex!

ABE: *(Dizzily)* First rest I've had since Basic.

RADIO: *(V O)* Don't fall asleep.

ABE: On this lovely hillside?

RADIO: *(V O)* Don't move! There's a sharp drop-off.

(ABE *looks down; sees he's at the edge of a cliff.*)

ABE: Yeah, I see.

RADIO: *(V O)* Apex, our procedures for this area don't allow...

ABE: Just get Benny out safe! I'm the leader. And fuck radio checks. I need a nap.

RADIO: *(V O)* Apex...!

(ABE *clicks off radio, tries to move*)

ABE: *(Pain)* Fucking hell.

GRAMMA: *(V O, intimate)* Thou preparest a table before me, in the presence of mine enemies.

ABE: *(Falling asleep)* That's nice, Gramma. But how 'bout you send me a Shabbat angel.

(GRAMMA's *hum, blending into music, rocks* ABE *to...*)

(*Time or dimension change—lights drop swiftly, music, nature sounds change to sunset*)

(*Sudden cracking through brush, off upstage.* ABE *pulls up abruptly, wincing at his quick move, but fired with adrenaline, and holding his Galil automatic rifle at ready.*)

(*More steps, crackling.* ABE, *expecting an approach, tries to move, can't, so lays low, but keeps rifle aimed upstage.*)

(Pause. Then a slight, khaki-dressed Arab—head swathed in a plain kaffiyeh—appears in upstage corner. ABE's rifle aims at the Arab, who pauses as after a long hike, lifts canteen for a drink.)

ABE: Halt.

(The Arab freezes, listening.)

ABE: Raise hands or I shoot.

(The Arab spins, dives toward ABE. ABE tries to fire but the Arab is already on top of him. He swings the rifle barrel against the Arab's legs, tripping him—)

SABRA: *(Angry yell)* Aaahh!

ABE: Gotcha! You son of a bitch!

(ABE lets his rifle swing on his back to grab the Arab, pull himself onto his knees, grapple fiercely, roll with his prey. Finally, by crushing with superior weight, ABE controls the Arab, reaches to tear at the kaffiyeh, and is astonished when long dark hair tumbles out.)

ABE: You're a girl?

(Taking advantage of his surprise, SABRA kicks him, wrenching away, and scrambling to her feet. ABE howls from the blow to his foot, but re-aims his weapon from where he sits, center.)

ABE: Stop! Or I shoot.

SABRA: Do it. Shoot me.

ABE: Come here.

(SABRA stands glaring at him, panting. ABE, who'll pass out if he steps on his foot, is like the lion trapped; SABRA, like the fox who stumbled on the trapped lion.)

ABE: Come here!

(She moves slowly to him.)

ABE: Give me your pack. *(Beat)* Give it! Slowly...

(She reluctantly slips off her knapsack, and lets it drop to the ground. As soon as she is within reach, he grabs her hand, twisting it and her arm upwards, so she drops to her knees.)

ABE: Now sit.

(Not satisfied, he pushes her forward onto her face.)

ABE: Get down!

(With his rifle jammed into her back, he dumps her pack. There's a map and a white dress heavily embroidered in red.)

ABE: Where's your weapons?

(No response. He jabs with the rifle, she yelps, but won't respond.)

ABE: Where are they?

SABRA: You're the killer.

(He roughly and thoroughly frisks her for weapons, but cannot rise from his knees.)

SABRA: *(Snarling)* Trespasser.

ABE: Yeah? And you're a fucking infiltrator.

SABRA: Sure.

(ABE has found a knife on her.)

ABE: What's this?

SABRA: For food, thief!

(Grabs her, shaking with his weak condition and frightened rage)

ABE: Benny's *blood* is all over your booby-trapped road. And you're fucking well going to pay!

(She spits at him.)

ABE: *(Grabbing her throat)* What are you doing here?

SABRA: *(Choking)* Get off my land!

ABE: Almost made it, didn't you? Only one more mile to the border. Where's your pals?

SABRA: Surrounding you.

(ABE pulls her roughly, close to him, like a shield.)

SABRA: Think I protect you? They'll shoot right through me.

(He twists her arm higher.)

SABRA: Aaaah!

ABE: Shut up!

(Silence. Both are panting heavily. ABE, on guard, expecting an attack, looks around.)

ABE: *(Long pause)* Maybe you are alone.

(She doesn't respond.)

ABE: Where are your weapons?

SABRA: What? My Kalashnikov? Grenade launcher? Pack of C-4? You think I've got nowhere to go? You think I'm a stinking *Palestinian*?

ABE: Who else.

SABRA: Ass among asses. *(Pulling them both toward the edge)* Careful, you'll fall. It's a long way down.

ABE: *(Pulling back on her)* What are you doing here?

SABRA: Tending my land! Afraid of heights? *(Pulling again)*

ABE: *(Pulling back on her)* You're trying to cross the border. To murder Jews!

SABRA: How. With my fists?

(She twists abruptly, flips him away, rises to jump from the ledge, while ABE *yells from the pain, and lights strobe as he fights for consciousness—)*

ABE: Don't jump!

(As she jumps, he begins a slide down the cliff, injured foot in air, rifle in hand, with both yelling; sound rises like siren— into Blackout—and out again, to reveal them both, landed at cliff's bottom, winded, looking up amazed at the cliff above them.)

SABRA: Hurt yourself?

ABE: *(Gasping, about to pass out)* Run. Go on!

SABRA: So you can shoot me?

ABE: *(Dizzy)* Why don't you run.

SABRA: Why should I. I'm home.

(She scrambles away, pulls vines [ropes] aside, and ABE *gasps.)*

ABE: *(Startled)* What is that?

SABRA: What do you think. A door.

ABE: A door in the hill? Come here!

SABRA: Scared?

(She moves toward him. As soon as she is close enough he grabs her, and twists her in front of him as a shield, but he stumbles back with the pain, and they fall together; he clings to her, but keeps the rifle trained on "the door." They sprawl there, with him panting.)

ABE: Who's in there.

(She looks at him with almost a smile, taunting, refusing to answer.)

ABE: *(Jerking her roughly)* What is this? Where are we!

(They struggle again, futilely, until he stops, panting from exhaustion.)

SABRA: *(Pause)* Want the key?

ABE: Key... Who are you?

SABRA: Or you'd rather blast it open. Purify it?

(He looks at her, not trusting.)

SABRA: Go ahead. Make it "pure." Kill everything in there. Then you're safe.

(ABE is unsure.)

SABRA: 'Course if there's ammunition behind this door, you fire, it explodes, and you've lost it.

ABE: *(Exhausted with pain, he snaps—)* Go.

SABRA: Go?

ABE: Slowly. To the door.

*(She approaches the door, glancing back at him.
He covers her with the rifle.)*

SABRA: Now what.

ABE: Open it. Slowly. If you make a fast move...

SABRA: ...you'll fire. I know the game. *(She unhooks the door)* Ready?

ABE: *(Pause, breathing hard, glaring at her, then—)* Open it.

(She pushes the door open, then stands aside, looking back at him. Nothing happens.)

ABE: Move in front of it.

*(She steps to the center of the opening, and looks at him.
He doesn't know what to do.)*

SABRA: Well?

ABE: *(Frustrated)* Come back here.

(She moves to him. When she's near, he swings her round, pulls himself up, and flings himself across her back; she staggers under the weight, but stays on her feet.)

ABE: Well, move!

(SABRA moves with ABE attached, dragging him toward the door. As they go through it, lights change, and sound/music cues GRAMMA's warm voice whispering...)

GRAMMA: *(V O)* Thou anointest my head with oil, my cup runneth over.

(... and they are inside the hill in a crude "field hut" dugout. Props may be real or mimed.)

ABE: I don't believe it. Where are we?

(SABRA slides ABE off of her onto the one sitting place.)

ABE: What is this place?

(SABRA stands looking at him.)

SABRA: Home.

ABE: What?

(Stand-off, like animals who've met in a clearing, on guard to learn who's dominant...then abruptly, she turns away—)

ABE: Wait...

(But she, gone to a pump or spring, ignores him, gets water in a pan, brings it, kneels in front of him, and lifts his bloodied foot onto her knees.)

ABE: *(Involuntarily yelping)* Aaaaah!

SABRA: It's filthy.

(She begins bathing his foot. It is a gentle ritual. When outside, SABRA displayed all the cunning and ferocity of a trapped animal—one as frightened as he—but once through the door a calm graciousness pervades her actions. He doesn't

resist, but watches her, breathing heavily, trying not to react to the pain.)

SABRA: Step on a land mine?

ABE: *(Grunting)* Damned terrorists.

SABRA: Wasn't theirs.

ABE: What do you know about it.

SABRA: You stepped on your own mine.

ABE: Fuck I did.

(She's reaching to get dirt from the deep center of the wound.)

SABRA: You Israelis drop mines around like cow cakes.

ABE: *(Gasping from sudden pain of where she's hit)* Ahhh.

SABRA: *(Examining the spot)* Not at all pretty.

(Pause while he recovers himself, watching her work)

ABE: Why were you crossing the security zone?

SABRA: *(Incredulous)* Security?

ABE: You know what it's called.

SABRA: Security, yes—for Jews. On my land!

ABE: That's right!

(Stand off. They stare belligerently at each other.)

ABE: Why were you crossing it?

(She goes back to working on his foot.)

SABRA: Came for the apples.

ABE: Apples...?

SABRA: You've left me no brothers to do it.

(ABE stares at her, uncertain whether to believe her.)

ABE: But, how did you...

SABRA: Get so far? Past your patrols, your snipers, your mines? This is Lebanon! You've no right to keep me out.

ABE: You must have...

SABRA: ...sneaked through. How else?

ABE: Why should I believe you?

SABRA: Because I felt safe, so you caught me.

ABE: I should believe you because I caught you?

SABRA: You never would have, not in a million years, if I hadn't felt safe.

(Finished bathing his foot, she drags a crate in front of him, and lifts the foot onto the crate.)

SABRA: *(Lifting)* I'm at home.

ABE: *(Pained by sudden movement)* Aaahh!

SABRA: Keep it up there. Unless you want it the size of your head.

(SABRA carries pan to the door, tosses bloody water out, goes back to draw a drink, carries it to ABE.)

(He watches her in the submissive silence of his awkward, necessarily obedient position, then drinks thirstily without taking his eyes off her, then says whimsically—)

ABE: Did my gramma maybe send you?

SABRA: Who?

ABE: My gramma. I asked her to send me a Shabbat angel.

(She looks at him, but, without responding, moves away, fills the pan again, lugs a sack from the corner, sits on the floor with pan and sack. ABE, watching her every move, and examining the surroundings, tries another tack—)

ABE: This isn't your home.

SABRA: No?

(She takes a potato from the sack, examines and discards it)

ABE: No. No one lives here.

SABRA: You *let* no one.

(She roughly dumps out several potatoes onto the floor)

ABE: This is just a field hut, a cave dug out of a hill. Where are you from?

(She looks at him, then returns to picking potatoes, dumping several into the pan of water. She will not respond.)

ABE: You said something about brothers. We'd left you no brothers?

(She doesn't look at him, but scrubs the potatoes ferociously. Music/sound He watches her, his eyes flutter, wanting to close, and in that state, he remembers the explosion. The vision floods over him, and he's reliving it, like a bad dream.)

ABE: *(Murmuring)* Benny...

(He snaps awake, as though with a whiff of ammonia, switches on his radio. It's his link with reality, but a reality so painful that he fears returning to it. Static buzz; SABRA spins, again, like a fearful animal. ABE sees her; they hold the look)

ABE: I won't hurt you.

(SABRA doesn't evade, watches him warily, a potato in hand, but ready to run. ABE, shaken by the radio-buzz's reality check, tries to reassure her.)

ABE: I'm sorry about the...searching you. I know that in your culture... Well, we have orders not to even touch you. I mean, if you're a girl. *(Beat)* Not that I wouldn't like to... I mean, it seems years since I've even seen a girl, so... But I wouldn't have been so rough, if... *(Gasps, suddenly back in the explosion)* I saw the mine exploding, and Benny on top of it, and... God, his leg was...

(ABE sees Benny with his leg blown off, then jerks himself out of the vision.)

ABE: So I'm not quite...normal. And I...nothing seems real, you know? I mean, I'm still here. But who are you? Sitting beside me. And what are you doing? *(Little laugh)* Preparing the meal for Shabbat?

(The radio crackles, and SABRA jumps, fearful.)

SABRA: Someone's coming for you?

(An all-channels bulletin interrupts her.)

RADIO: *(V O)* Command to all channels. Headquarters under attack from unidentified Hezbollah positions north. We're receiving heavy incoming mortar and R P G fire. Returning patrol squads proceed only under advisement. Repeat. Proceed to base only under advisement.

ABE: *(Sudden extreme fear, like unexpected tears—)* God! Did you get Benny through?

SABRA: *(Warily watching)* Someone's coming for you?

ABE: *(Calming himself)* Probably.

(His attention is pulled back to her; he watches for a reponse, but she hides again in potato cleaning. Wearily, he lets the rifle slide and props it behind his shoulder.)

ABE: *(Casually)* 'Course they're coming.

(SABRA is alert, stealthily watching him.)

ABE: *(Trying to tease)* Think they'd leave me alone out here? With a stream of Jew-hating infiltrators?

(In one sudden move, she's up and bolting for the door. He clumsily twists to grab his rifle.)

ABE: *(Startled)* Wait! You can't...

(Two simultaneous actions: 1. ABE, swinging his foot down, sways dizzily, collapses to floor.)

ABE: Shit!

*(2. SABRA hesitates outside, considering his call, then races
to "climb the cliff." Outside, sound/music. SABRA starts
scramble up hill, ABE drags himself to shelter by the door.
GRAMMA's voice hums in the wind, and SABRA hears—)*

SABRA: *(Awed, but fearless)* Who are you?

*(Then SABRA suddenly sees—with a music clash—
ABE's exploded, bloody boot caught in a vine. She reaches
for the boot, holds it, looks back toward ABE, and returns,
gathering firewood on her way.)*

RADIO: *(V O)* Command to all channels. All combat
ready units, report immediately.

*(ABE is collapsed, on alert for an attack, next to door.
SABRA comes through door, meets his rifle barrel,
which he holds on her an instant, then deflects, embarrassed,
while she just looks at him.)*

ABE: Welcome home.

*(She moves straight in, dumps firewood, and turns,
holding bloodied remains of his boot towards him.
It shocks him, but he bounces back on the next breath.)*

ABE: How about that. My boot. Wherever I step,
you'll make blood soup. Won't you.

(They look at each other.)

ABE: That's a joke. Like my gramma would say.
Not funny?

SABRA: Who?

ABE: You heard me.

*(She stares at him, then bends, lets him lean across her,
and drags him back to the seat.)*

ABE: *(Gasping, as they move)* Aw...you're just pissed you can't get two good boots. Right? You'd trade for a Seiko diver's watch. Or a couple ounces of hash.

(She dumps him back onto the seat. He gazes up at her.)

ABE: What are you up to?

(She simply holds his boot out toward him. As he reaches for it, she notices something protruding from its torn lining. She takes hold, and draws out a flat piece of metal on a string.)

ABE: Extra dog-tags.

(She looks at him quizzically.)

ABE: In case you blow my head off. In case you want to know who my feet used to belong to.

(They hold their look for an instant, then she drops the tag in his lap and returns to her firewood.)

ABE: Not even curious? *(He picks up the tag, looks at it, reads.)* "Abraham Arik Mannheim. 2nd Lieutenant. 9665379, Type O."

(He looks at her, but she's paying no attention, building a fire.)

ABE: Never know when it'll come in handy. *(Beat)*
You don't think so? You don't want my dogtags?
You could trade 'em for a dozen prisoners.
We're crazy like that. We care about our people. *(Pause. He's getting angry.)* This is everyday business out here. Blood and corpses. You shouldn't be running lose!

(No response from her)

ABE: Listen. You don't want to be found out. You don't want to meet my buddies, right? You've been lucky so far. But I should have shot you on sight.

SABRA: *(Sudden, sharp)* Is that my fault?

ABE: *(Angry)* I'm talking reality, not rights. It's not my fault either, but I could have shot you. And that's just my orders. To protect *me!*

(He glares at her, but when she doesn't challenge, he calms, watches her lighting fire)

ABE: Sure you know how to do that?

(She glances at him, and goes on with her work.)

ABE: I mean, my sister wouldn't have the least idea...

(The fire catches. SABRA puts the pan over it, then turns, looking at him oddly.)

ABE: Yes. I have a sister. *(Now that he has her attention, he presses.)* Did you hear what I said?

(Ignoring the question, she steps toward him, and stands in front of him without speaking.)

ABE: What?

SABRA: *(Pause)* My knife.

ABE: *(Puzzled an instant, then—)* Oh. Sure. Sure.

(He reaches into a pocket, grunting with the pain of moving, retrieves her knife, then holds it, making her wait)

ABE: Your eyes talk anyway. *(Beat)* At home Mama told me, "if you want something, use your mouth." But your eyes are talking. If I could just...translate.

(He hands her the knife.)

ABE: They look a hundred years deep.

(She looks at him, holding the utility knife in her hand. She opens it, still standing, looking at him. He refuses to be intimidated.)

ABE: *(Softly, with wonder)* What happened to you?

(She holds the look an instant longer, then suddenly moves back to the potatoes, slices them into heating water.)

ABE: When you did talk, you lied.

(She glances at him, a bit startled.)

ABE: About what you're doing here. Doesn't figure.
Too much risk. Your life for a few apples?

(She's uneasy, but doesn't respond.)

ABE: Got you, huh?

SABRA: Maybe it's...a gesture.

ABE: Sneaking in here?

SABRA: So the land won't forget me.

*(She's motionless, speaking quietly. He watches her,
trying to follow.)*

SABRA: Just touching it. As though, if I don't visit,
it'll be lost.

ABE: *(As still as she, moved)* You're beautiful now...
naked. You're a child.

SABRA: *(Wanting to elude the intimacy, but caught)*
What difference does that make.

ABE: But old enough to have a husband.

SABRA: A girl can choose. Whether to...

ABE: I thought it was "arranged" for her.

SABRA: In civilization it is. We live in disaster.

ABE: People still live.

(They look at each other; the radio crackles. Both jump)

RADIO: *(V O)* Dog-star to Apex. Dog-star to Apex.

*(She retreats, her focus on the radio, as though it's a bomb.
ABE watches her fright. For him, the radio is like a kick in
his gut, and the horrifying reality of Benny sweeps back.)*

ABE: *(Tense)* Abe here. How's Benny?

RADIO: *(V O. Through static, evasive)* We just got through. The shelling's awful here.

ABE: I've got interference...what?

RADIO: *(V O)* I said the shelling...

ABE: How's Benny!

RADIO: *(V O)* We...got him into emergency. He bled a lot, Apex, he...

ABE: What did the medics say!

RADIO: *(V O)* They're gonna see if they can sew him up.

ABE: *(Not believing it)* Sure.

RADIO: *(V O)* How are you doing?

ABE: *(Near tears)* Great. Great.

RADIO: *(V O)* You know we're under attack here.

ABE: I heard.

RADIO: *(V O)* Soon as it eases up, we'll find an A P C and be out after you.

ABE: I'll be here. Out.

(Radio clicks off. Drained, ABE looks at SABRA, gauging her fear.)

SABRA: They'll be coming.

ABE: They're under fire.

SABRA: But they'll be coming.

ABE: They're not coming yet.

SABRA: Then I'll go.

ABE: Go? You can't go.

SABRA: Yes. You'll let me.

ABE: *(Light, trying to tease)* Let you go? When I've got such a nurse-maid?

SABRA: Let me go.

ABE: You're free. You went for wood. You could run.

SABRA: You could shoot.

ABE: Yeah.

(She looks at him, considering—will he fire?—then gathers her pack, eyes on him the whole time, and, still facing him, edges toward door. She is going to run. But as she steps into doorway, he points the rifle at her, and flips off the safety. She stops, caught.)

SABRA: You said I was free.

ABE: *(Beat)* But I'm not.

(She still stands poised to run. He doesn't back down.)

ABE: Are your potatoes boiling?

(She looks at the fire, but stays stubbornly in the door. He keeps the rifle on her.)

ABE: Why did you do all this?

SABRA: What.

ABE: Take care of me.

SABRA: *(Beat)* Arab hospitality.

ABE: For a Jew?

SABRA: *(Shrugs)* Anyone.

ABE: An invader?

SABRA: All right. I was lulling you. Till you fall asleep.

ABE: *(Smiling)* To see that, you'll have to stay.

(She huffs, frustrated, wanting with every ounce to be gone, holds a beat, then flings down her pack, and moves back to fire. ABE lowers rifle, watches her a minute, then salutes cheerfully.)

ABE: Hi, I'm Abe.

(She looks at him blankly.)

ABE: You have a name?

(She shakes her head.)

ABE: You don't?

SABRA: You've taken it.

ABE: Your name?

SABRA: Who I am. Everything.

ABE: *(Lightly)* So you are my nameless captive.
Or I'm yours. I mean, you could kill me... *(Snaps his fingers)* ...like that. Being female and clever and all.

(She makes no response.)

ABE: But maybe you don't want to make a mess.

SABRA: I want you gone.

ABE: Not simple.

SABRA: Just let me go back.

ABE: Back where?

SABRA: The way I came.

ABE: You're not that stupid! It's possible, just possible, if you're very careful where you step, to make it through these woods...in daylight. But at dark, they start to move.

(She is affected, watches him.)

ABE: And now it's dark. And now...a deadly stream comes slipping, probing, pouring through—all terrorists. You know that, don't you. All ripe with blood lust. They don't care who they kill. Just so it's Jews. But we Jews are out here too. Every single night, in a new place, a new nest, we wait for them to come, we pick them off, they don't get through alive.

(Pause, as he stares at her)

ABE: So. You want to go out and take up sides?

(She meets his stare, but doesn't speak. He, angry at her stubborness, is winding into a rage.)

ABE: We have machines that find you if you move. Or even if you don't. In daylight, I ask myself questions, a whole rule-book full, before I shoot you, but not at night. At night whatever moves is killed. *(Beat)* And it's getting worse. They're coming younger, they're coming loaded with explosives, they're coming on purpose to die. Kamakazis. Human bombs. You'd like to scoot out there and smack into one of them? Kids, with glassy eyes, looking to get to heaven?

SABRA: It's not heaven they want. You took their land.

ABE: You ready to join them? *(Beat)* Are you!?

(She won't answer.)

ABE: If you think you're safe out there, you must have friends I haven't met.

(She turns away.)

ABE: And what if the only reason your friends don't attack...is that I'm holding you?

SABRA: *(Derisive)* Tsaa.

ABE: Wrong?

SABRA: You'd be dead.

ABE: They'd sacrifice you to get at me?

SABRA: I'm alone!

ABE: *(Little smile)* Not...anymore.

(She shoots a look at him. He meets it, then smiles broadly.)

ABE: I'm hungry.

(Frustrated, she lets out an expletive, but goes back to tending the potatoes. ABE watches her.)

ABE: What are you afraid of?

SABRA: Nothing.

ABE: The other soldiers? Me?

SABRA: Nothing. *(Suddenly icy, direct)* There's nothing you can do...would make me afraid.

ABE: *(Pause)* Why did you bathe my foot?

(She looks at him without answering.)

ABE: Why?

SABRA: It looked stupid.

ABE: Stupid? Hmh. Guess so.

(Unable to see in the late dusk, she gets a stick-end burning, brings a lantern, and lights it.)

ABE: Candles at sundown. Nice. *(Pause)* Want some flavoring...for your potato stew?

SABRA: What?

ABE: There's bully beef. In my bag.

(She looks at his bag, and back at him, swallows hungrily.)

ABE: It won't bite. It's de-horned.

(She moves to the bag, extracts tin of beef, looks at him. He suddenly switches from teasing to quiet pleading—)

ABE: My silent Arab angel...we're only here because of the Palestinians. To keep them away from the border. The infiltrators. They're violating your country too.

(He puts out his hand for the tin. She hands it to him. He extracts an P-2 opener, opens the tin. She's watching him steadily. He sniffs the can)

ABE: Mmmh. Smell this.

(She ignores what he's saying, takes the tin, continues to look at him.)

SABRA: Just let me go.

ABE: You're afraid to face the soldiers.

SABRA: Don't you know what they'll do?

ABE: We'll have a great time.

SABRA: *(Shocked)* What?

ABE: If you're who you say you are.

SABRA: They'll put me in prison. They'll destroy this place. They'll...

ABE: You think we're barbaric?

SABRA: I don't give it a name. I see what you do.

(He absorbs the sting, then sends back cold steel—)

ABE: How much could you get for me? Live. From Hezbollah?

(She reacts with a hiss, and angrily moves back to dump the beef into the potatoes. Conversation over. Stony silence)

(ABE continues watching her, sorry he cut off the talking. He adjusts the rifle, checking to see whether she's paying attention. She isn't. Finally he shifts, and yelps in pain. She looks his way, but doesn't respond. He moves again, gasping. She looks at him. He sees he has her attention.)

ABE: I think it's drying too much. I...

SABRA: Have you got an undershirt?

ABE: What?

SABRA: An undershirt.

ABE: Yes.

SABRA: Take it off.

(He props himself, watching her quizzically, and unbuttons his shirt. She's moving with two plates of food. He waits with his eyes on her, to remove his undershirt when she can watch

him. She puts the plates down beside him, then straightens, watching him. He takes off his undershirt)

ABE: Well?

(She puts her hand out for the undershirt, takes it, and with quick jerks, tears it into broad strips. Then she goes to his kit without asking, searches in it, and brings out a tube of ointment, smears it lightly on his foot, then lifts and wraps the foot, gently. ABE *bears all this in silence, his eyes on her every move, until—)*

ABE: You're very...effective.

SABRA: *(Her eyes flash.)* I've had practice. *(She continues wrapping.)*

ABE: You've done this before?

SABRA: More times than you dream of.

ABE: *(Quiet, earnest)* Tell me.

(She looks at him. Her face is open again; she wants to tell him, but the radio crackles. She jumps, but he puts out his hand, and makes the radio wait—)

ABE: Are you sure...we're enemies?

RADIO: *(V O)* Dog-star to Apex. Dog-star to Apex.

(She looks at the radio, back at him, then moves away.)

ABE: Apex here. *(He breathes deep before asking)* How's Benny.

RADIO: *(V O. Beat, then, evading the question)* Can you verify your coordinates, Apex?

ABE: How's Benny?

RADIO: *(V O)* We have you at 33.16 north, 35.32.5 east. That's roughly 11 kilometers from Beaufort Castle.

ABE: *(Trying to hold in his panic)* How's Benny?

RADIO: *(V O)* We're, uh, responding to incoming fire. We haven't been able to...

ABE: Answer me about Benny!

RADIO: *(V O)* He's out of surgery, Apex. But nobody can see him. It...doesn't look good.

ABE: Oh, god. Oh, god.

RADIO: *(V O)* Damn, Apex. Don't make me sorry I told you.

ABE: I'd have killed you if you didn't.

RADIO: *(V O)* Verify, Apex. Are those your coordinates. We've located an A P C. We're going to crash on through.

(ABE's head is hanging, bent over the radio. Pause)

RADIO: *(V O)* Apex? Do you read me? We're coming after you.

(ABE slowly lifts his head, looks at SABRA, who's watching him like a cornered animal.)

ABE: There's...no need.

RADIO: *(V O)* What?

ABE: Don't risk it. Not at night. I...found shelter.

RADIO: *(V O)* What shelter? Apex. Are you all right?

ABE: Just...start out in the morning.

RADIO: *(V O)* What about your foot?

ABE: *(Pause)* I washed it. *(Beat)* O K?

RADIO: *(V O)* Apex...I don't think...

ABE: I just need to keep it elevated. Out.

(ABE clicks off radio, breathing hard, wanting to push away the pain of Benny, he looks at SABRA.)

ABE: Did you poison it? *(Reaches for his plate, watching her, smells it)* Uumm. Delectable poison.

(SABRA stands looking at him.)

ABE: Come. Sit by me. Eat.

(She doesn't move, but continues looking at him.)

ABE: Among Jews the women may now sit at table. Though not at prayer. Will you come?

SABRA: *(Not moving)* You didn't tell them.

ABE: Tell them what?

SABRA: About me. About this dangerous infiltrator.

ABE: They might not sleep well, knowing.

SABRA: And you will?

ABE: *(Looks at her; beat)* Is that a warning?

(For the first time, it seems, she smiles. Then, though still wary, she comes, takes up her plate, kneels near him on the floor, to eat. ABE closes his eyes, says a blessing. She watches, then quickly, as he finishes, crosses herself.)

ABE: What's that?

SABRA: What.

ABE: You're not Muslim.

SABRA: Why do you ask.

ABE: You're Christian.

SABRA: What difference?

ABE: You crossed yourself.

SABRA: I'm Arab.

(He looks at her, puzzled. She begins eating, hungrily. ABE tries, but has little appetite. They continue throughout to watch each other. When she finishes, she's breathing hard from the fast eating. And still watching him. Pause)

SABRA: He's your friend.

ABE: Who?

SABRA: *(Beat)* Benny.

(ABE *looks at her, surprised at her noticing, but then tight, bitter—)*

ABE: Will it make a difference?

SABRA: A difference?

ABE: In whether you hope he dies?

SABRA: *(Beat)* Have you seen anyone die.

ABE: *(Startled, he holds her look, then lets spill—)* He's my best friend. We joined up together. He and my sister are... *(Breaks off, choked. Pause)*

SABRA: *(Soft, but noncommital)* Death is easy.

ABE: He was teasing me, you know? We were on opposite sides of the road, plodding behind the Bedouin, the tracker, focused on the ditch, for anything—wires, barrels, trash—anything signifying "bomb here." But Benny stops... Telling me he's spotted a yellow-bill. He's such a goof. He won't believe in danger. And we have this standing bet—whoever spots a yellow...
He must've been standing on the thing already, right on it. And I got close, knocked into him deflected him just a bit, and... It was so loud. Then, just a ringing sound, like my ear drum had snapped, before I remember him slipping down next to me, his guts a mess, and his leg...gone. Oh, God. *(Doubles over, can't say more)*

SABRA: It might've been worse.

ABE: What?

SABRA: If you hadn't taken...part of the force of it.

ABE: You know what a blast does to flesh? The way it flings everything, bursts, just like a... *(Realizes)* You do know. You know everything, don't you?

(He takes her hand. She looks at him, startled, attempts to withdraw her hand, but—)

ABE: Don't...move. Don't be afraid. What can I do? I can't run after you.

(She sits still, watching him warily.)

ABE: What does this do? Does this compromise you? Are you defiled if I hold your hand? What's going to happen here. O K. You want me to let you go? Tell me who you are.

(He waits. She doesn't respond.)

ABE: It's easy. "Abe, my name is Nadia. I come from..." Wrong? Is your name not Nadia?

SABRA: *(Pause)* Sabra.

ABE: Sabra? That's not a name. Is it? Sabra? All right, all right, it's a start. You're Sabra. And you can't live here now, but you live...where? Beirut?

(He looks in her eyes, and she looks at him, but doesn't answer.)

ABE: That's it? You've come all the way from Beirut? Why won't you tell me?

(First she just shakes her head, then says calmly—)

SABRA: I don't exist.

ABE: You don't exist. You're some spirit of the woods. I'm imagining you?

SABRA: Maybe you are.

ABE: Well. Something brought you here. There's some reason you're "visiting" me.

SABRA: No...

ABE: No?

SABRA: Why are you here?

ABE: Me? Dumb luck.

SABRA: Luck?

ABE: Sooner or later, it runs out. That's what they tell you.

SABRA: Runs out.

ABE: And that's when you step on a mine. Whammo.

(The joke ABE was making turns on him; the "whammo" becomes Benny being blown up. He lets out a contorted cry, but comes out of it gasping, having found a reason it happened—)

ABE: It's because Benny was "short"—only four days till he'd go home—that's when you let down, when you dream you're out of it, next step to being free—and he pulled me along into his dreaming, just like...God. This whole thing is fatal. I can believe you don't exist. And you conjured this place, just to trip my reflex— "Let go. You're safe home."

I'm out here forty days at a time, and every minute of every hour of those forty, I keep a vision of my death, moving with me, clear. I have to. Because I'll never see my waiting death...before it comes. And I have to stay alive. So my eyes are dry, on constant alert, sweeping, with my head on my taut neck. "Don't blink. Don't let down. Catch anything that moves."

Could you do that? On a warm summer night...it's impossible. Spread out for ambush, lying in the grass, impossible. It gets so clear, so soft. The star fires so close overhead. How can I keep death alive inside me?

(ABE stops. SABRA's gazing at him. Embarrassed at revealing himself, ABE asks abruptly—)

ABE: What do your parents say about you?

SABRA: *(Averting her gaze)* My parents.

ABE: Yes. Is this—what you're up to—proper behavior for a fine young Arab of good...

(He stops himself, seeing her look.)

SABRA: I don't have any.

ABE: No parents?

SABRA: *(Looks at him)* It was a bomb. In a car.

ABE: And that's why you don't exist?

SABRA: *(Shakes her head, vaguely)* No. I never existed.

ABE: Sabra. Your brothers. You said...

SABRA: They weren't really my brothers. They're Um Sa'ad's sons.

ABE: *(Glad to have an answer he can translate)* Um Sa'ad. The mother of Sa'ad. She raised you?

(SABRA looks at him with quiet eyes)

ABE: *(Satisfied to have an answer)* Well. That's something.

SABRA: How many Arabs have you killed?

ABE: None. None! Sabra, listen. I asked for this.
I transferred here, out of Israel, so I wouldn't wind up killing children! I don't like this. You think I want to kill someone? I don't hate Arabs. I only want to live in peace. But they keep on coming to kill us.
   And I'll tell you, it's not like you think. They've got no chance here. No chance to win. To even fight. I've seen it work. One night on ambush, I crawled back to the A P C, the tank, and inside, they're watching with a night-scope, on a screen, like a video cartoon! And there come the stick creatures. They show up on the screen because they're alive out there, they're warm, they're moving—not even close, a whole kilometer away! And

because it's night, we don't ask—we just fire. We fire,
several rounds, and every shell seeks warmth, and
bursts itself in flesh. We watch. In silence...the creatures
falter on the screen. No shrieks. Nothing. The stick
shapes just begin to fade, getting dimmer as their
warmth is lost, until they blank out, blending with
the screen, completely cold. *(Pause)* No. I've never
seen anyone die.

SABRA: *(Darkly)* Lucky.

ABE: *(Shouts)* I'm protecting the border, farmers two
kilometers from here! Am I allowed to defend my
home?!

*(His outburst strikes her strangely. She looks at him, open,
like a child.)*

SABRA: Home. Yes. *(Beat)* What's it like.

ABE: I... What?

SABRA: Your home.

ABE: My home.

SABRA: Yes. You have one?

ABE: Of course!

SABRA: What's it like.

ABE: It's... What do you mean?

SABRA: A house. A farm?

ABE: Just a house. A...

SABRA: On a hill?

ABE: Well... Yes, a hill.

SABRA: Is there a tree?

ABE: What are you after?

SABRA: It's old, isn't it.

ABE: *(Amused)* I don't understand.

SABRA: *(Asking him to imagine himself there)* You're at home. You see your mother. Your father. A rug by the door. A picture of your sister and you—but younger.

ABE: *(Seeing his home)* Yes...

SABRA: Are you afraid?

ABE: At home? No.

SABRA: No one is?

ABE: My gramma.

SABRA: She's afraid?

ABE: My mother was born in a camp...in Germany.

SABRA: A camp? With no sewer.

ABE: No, I think...I think they had a sewer.

SABRA: She was afraid.

ABE: Yes.

SABRA: So then, in the camp with her baby—your gramma had no home.

ABE: No, then she didn't. And later...

SABRA: Did someone take it? Did she fight?

ABE: It wasn't exactly...

SABRA: You have to fight. It's your home.

ABE: Yes.

SABRA: If they come in the night. Where it's safe. Where your mother holds you. Where you go to sleep.

ABE: *(Alarmed)* Sabra. What is it? What happened.

(She stops, looks at him, her eyes hurting.)

ABE: How old were you.

SABRA: How old?

ABE: When your parents were killed.

SABRA: Old. Plenty old.

ABE: How many years?

SABRA: *(Without emotion)* Eight.

(ABE swallows hard, and, not knowing what to say, covers his readiness to cry with whimsy, wanting to make her smile.)

ABE: And here you are...apple hunting—a spirit in the woods, who's snatched me, this unsuspecting soldier, a spirit...who doesn't even exist.

(She only looks at him.)

ABE: Does Um Sa'ad tell stories?

SABRA: Stories?

ABE: Yes. Good stories.

SABRA: Not now.

ABE: But before.

SABRA: Sometimes. About a bird.

ABE: Tell me.

(She looks far away.)

ABE: Don't go.

SABRA: I'm not.

ABE: Yes, you did. You raised your wings.

SABRA: No.

ABE: You left. You tried.

(She looks at him.)

ABE: You're my captive here. You have to stay in my good graces. I want to see this hand.

(He takes her hand, turns it to look at her palm.)

ABE: Aha. You know what I see here? In this line here.
(Tracing it) This life line...

SABRA: I don't have any.

ABE: Ah ah ah, let me look. What I see is a good hand,
a strong one. It dreams. It feels...many things. It needs
to build a strong life. I have hold of it here, you see?
It does exist.

*(She looks at him. Her mouth opens, but no sound comes.
Suddenly she weeps, hard, bends over weeping. He's startled,
nearly weeps himself, puts his arm around her. She sobs,
clings to his arm.)*

ABE: Don't. Don't, don't, Sabra. It's all right.

*(He leans over, kisses her hair. Then kisses her cheek. She
breathes deep, catching her breath, realizes what's happening,
raises her head to look in his face, questioningly.)*

ABE: I'm sorry. I...

*(He stops speaking, goes on looking at her as she gazes at
him. Then, suddenly, she leans forward and kisses him
child-like, then pulls back to look at him. He smiles.)*

ABE: Well. Thank you. That...I'm sure that did happen.

*(She leans forward again, and kisses him a bit longer, then
pulls back to look at him. She reaches her hand to touch his
face, curiously. Watching her, silent, he takes her hand from
his face, and kisses it, several times, all over, still watching
her. She leans forward again, and, instantly they are holding
and kissing each other.)*

ABE: Don't hurt, don't hurt, please don't hurt so much.

(They go on kissing until she pulls back, catching a breath)

SABRA: I'm your enemy.

ABE: Yes. Yes, you are. *(Kisses her gently)*

SABRA: Why did you come here?

ABE: To be with you.

(They kiss again until she suddenly puts her hand over his mouth, and averts her head to listen, alarmed. Sound in night—could be natural or music—)

SABRA: Shhhh. *(Douses lantern, darts to door, listens)* It may be nothing. *(Pause, listening)* If it's your soldiers...

ABE: They'd warn me first. How about yours? More, uh, apple farmers?

(She shoots a look at him, but doesn't answer the challenge.)

ABE: For all I know, we're sitting on the main road to the promised land.

SABRA: What would happen to you if...

ABE: If what.

SABRA: What would your Captain say? About me.

ABE: If he found me with you? Dumb luck.

(She turns away to the door.)

ABE: I'm teasing, Sabra. Come here.

SABRA: It's dark.

ABE: Yes. It's dark now. No one can find us. Come here.

(She stands watching him.)

ABE: Yes. You're right. I'd be in giant trouble. Even for talking, let alone...touching.

(Satisfied, she moves back to sit beside him.)

ABE: So, my Shabbat angel, tell me your story.

(She looks away.)

ABE: This is not fair, you know. I don't even know your name.

(She looks at him.)

ABE: Sabra isn't your name.

SABRA: Abraham.

ABE: That's mine.

SABRA: Abraham.

ABE: How about your "brother", Sa'ad?

SABRA: Yes.

ABE: Um Sa'ad's first born. What happened to him?

SABRA: He went to the fighting. She wanted him to be a priest. But he went to the fight.

ABE: What fight?

(She looks at him, and away)

ABE: Against Israelis? He's with one of the factions?

SABRA: No more. Shot through the throat. *(Pause)* She says she gives them. It's all she can do. She gives sons.

ABE: And the other?

SABRA: Hamid.

ABE: Hamid.

SABRA: He'd curl my hair round his finger.

ABE: Hamid is...

(She bites her lip, turns away.)

ABE: Tell me.

SABRA: Hamid studied to doctor. He didn't believe in the fighting.

ABE: Then what.

SABRA: *(Simply, without emotion)* Your soldiers took him anyway. They must have thought he knew... would tell...about his brother. So they tried to make him. They beat him every day, they beat him on the head until...his eye was crushed, and then, so no more marks would show, they hanged him naked by his wrists. They piped in screeching, screams of others, and wouldn't let him sleep. They made him crawl and bark.

ABE: No...please...

SABRA: They cut his feet. They...

ABE: Stop, please...

SABRA: ...did things to his sex, it was...

ABE: That's enough.

SABRA: *(Pause)* He didn't ever sign their paper. But when they let him out, before he died he told Um Sa'ad—they were so strong, they must be right, he wished he were a Jew.

(ABE's *head goes back, mouth open without a sound, then drops forward)*

ABE: I can't believe this, Sabra. When was this.

SABRA: *(Dry)* He came home blind. Then he died. That I saw.

(Breathing deep, ABE *calms himself, then looks at her, determined to go on.)*

ABE: Before. When you were only eight...did you have real brothers or sisters?

*(*SABRA *gets up swiftly to move away, but he holds her hand to stop her.)*

ABE: Sabra:

(She stands silent.)

ABE: I'll stop asking. Sit with me.

(She stays standing.)

ABE: Please don't be afraid of me.

SABRA: *(Softly, a vow)* Your name shall be Abraham...
for a father of many nations have I made thee.

ABE: Yes. That's what they say. *(Little laugh)* And I try to
understand it.

SABRA: *(Gaining strength)* And the angel of the Lord
called unto him out of heaven, saying "Abraham.
Abraham." And he said "Here I am."

*(She slowly extends her hand to him, and he takes it,
carefully)*

SABRA: Where do you come from, Abraham?

ABE: Jerusalem.

(Startled, she breathes a cry of joy)

SABRA: No...!

ABE: I do. Have you seen it?

SABRA: *(Her mouth opens without speaking, then—)* No.

ABE: But everyone knows...

SABRA: Yes. Everyone knows Jerusalem.

ABE: You have to come. You have to see it. The great
mosque is brilliant, so...breathtaking, cut out of the blue
sky.

SABRA: *(Shyly)* And the air rings?

ABE: *(Laughs)* It does! It's so clear.

SABRA: *(Slowly smiling. A glow begins to warm her.)*
Everyone comes from Jerusalem.

ABE: Yes. When you're there, you know. All of
Abraham's children.

*(He's troubled, feels like weeping, so he smiles and reaches for
her. But she holds back, wanting to tell him something.)*

SABRA: *(An excitement beginning)* This night is like no
other.

ABE: *(Laugh)* That's for sure.

SABRA: You don't understand, but you will. I...

ABE: You can tell me.

(She shakes her head, unable to go on. He just wants her close to him.)

ABE: Then come. Tell me the bird story.

SABRA: What story?

ABE: About the bird.

SABRA: That Um Sa'ad tells?

ABE: Yes.

SABRA: It just learns to fly.

ABE: *(Smiling)* That's all?

(As she begins, ABE draws her until she's sitting close to him. She tells it like a child.)

SABRA: The bird is born in a terrible desert, ugly and full of screams. But the bird has a dream of an olive tree, and awakes thinking she's lost, because the dream—an old stone wall with eggplants growing, and strawberries along its foot, and at its end, a silver, rustling, olive tree—is filling her mind, until she believes that this is real, and the ugly iron desert full of terrible cries is the dream.
    So she tells herself "If you could only fly, you could lift out of this dream and find the sweet, warm, real world." And she begins to try. First she just runs. And runs, and runs, along the sharp edge, flapping her flimsy wings, until she feels a bit of strength seeping across her back and out to the pinions. Then one day when she runs and flaps till she's dizzy, she forgets to stop—and keeps on flapping out past the edge and into the sky. *(She stops, and sits silent.)*

ABE: Does she find it?

SABRA: What.

ABE: The dream.

SABRA: Which dream?

ABE: The one with the olive tree.

SABRA: No, it's real.

ABE: Does she find it?

SABRA: I don't know.

ABE: You don't?

SABRA: I always fall asleep in the clouds.

ABE: Ahhh.

(She smiles suddenly, like sun coming out, then looks at him, shyly.)

SABRA: Are you married, Abraham?

ABE: Me?

SABRA: Are you married?

ABE: *(Laughing)* No.

SABRA: Good.

ABE: Yes. That's lucky.

SABRA: But you are...a man.

ABE: What?

(She doesn't repeat the question, but averts her eyes.)

ABE: Am I a man? *(Realizing she means sexually)* Well, yes. Yes.

SABRA: Good. *(Beat)* Because I'm going to love you.

ABE: What.

(She looks at him an instant, then rises, gets a quilt, and spreads it on the floor in front of him. He watches, not able to believe he heard right.)

ABE: Sabra...

SABRA: *(On her knees, looking at him)* Come.

ABE: I don't...

SABRA: You don't what?

ABE: I don't know what...

SABRA: But will you be happy?

ABE: When?

SABRA: When I love you?

ABE: Yes! But Sabra...

SABRA: *(Rising to let him lean on her)* Then come.

(She puts her arm around him, and lifts. He rises, then slides as she lowers him, gently, onto the quilt. She makes him comfortable, may loosen his clothing.)

ABE: You're teasing me. You aren't serious.

SABRA: Oh yes. Very serious. This night is important to me, Abraham. I don't expect you to understand.

ABE: *(Ironic)* Oh, I understand how important this is. That's why...

SABRA: Don't you want me, Abraham?

ABE: Yes! Yes, I do.

SABRA: Good.

ABE: But have you...?

SABRA: Have I what?

ABE: Have you...loved someone before?

(She smiles warmly at him, speaks emphatically, as though taking a vow.)

SABRA: No, Abraham.

(He perplexed, stares at her.)

ABE: Well then, we can't!

SABRA: No?

(Kneeling beside him, with a shy intake of breath, she begins to unbutton her shirt.)

ABE: *(Whispers)* No... *(Shouts)* Sabra, stop it!

SABRA: Don't be afraid, Abraham. *(Reassuring)* You came to me from Jerusalem.

ABE: But your father your brother... You have uncles?

(She kisses him. She undoes her pants, pulls them off, kneels in her underpants.)

ABE: Sabra, you know better. They'll kill you.

SABRA: Shhhh. It won't hurt your foot.

(He pulls her to him, kisses her breasts. She watches him, touching his hair, then kisses him, and bends to unbutton his pants.)

ABE: Sabra, we can't. A woman who shames her family can be killed.

SABRA: It's no shame. No shame.

ABE: Listen to me.

SABRA: You lie, Abraham. You're ready. You want to come into me.

(She leans to kiss him. He pulls her on top of him.)

ABE: Oh my god.

SABRA: If I promise you. I promise you no one will know. You want me. Help me. Show me how. It's just once.

(They kiss hungrily, until he stops abruptly.)

ABE: What makes you think I know how?

SABRA: *(Sits up with startled cry—)* Abraham!

ABE: *(Ready to be defensive)* What.

SABRA: You don't? You've never loved someone?

ABE: No I haven't, but that's not what matters here.

SABRA: Yes, yes, it does. It's perfect!

ABE: Please, Sabra, we have to stop.

(But they go on, neither wanting or trying to stop.)

SABRA: It can't hurt me, Abraham. It's life. Just once,
I want life.

(Lights fade to nearly black.)

*(In the dark, SABRA slides to lying beside ABE. Pause.
Night sounds. Israeli folk theme. ABE, thinking he hears
something, starts awake.)*

ABE: *(Groggy)* Gramma? Are you here?

GRAMMA: *(VO. Intimate, teasing, wise—)* Never mind,
Abraham, I know what you want to tell me.

ABE: *(Embarrassed to be caught sleeping with SABRA)*
But not now.

*(GRAMMA, at ease, as though picking up in the middle of a
conversation, chatty, wondering—)*

GRAMMA: *(V O)* A boxcar slamming shut. That's what
I remember—that sound. The dark. I'll never forget.
With your grandfather still outside. And your mother
kicking me from inside...oh, Abraham. The bottomless
hell that was coming I didn't imagine, but I knew...
that slam was the end of life. But you know, Abraham,
after all...it wasn't.

ABE: Right.

*(As GRAMMA hums, ABE reaches for SABRA, she rolls to
him, and they sleep.)*

(Dim streak of light, not yet dawn. SABRA raises her head. The two are entwined. ABE half-wakes, holding her, but she murmurs to him —)

SABRA: It's nothing. I have to go behind a bush. Sleep, my Abraham.

(He lets her slide away from him. She goes to the door, opens it, looks back at ABE, sees he's sleeping. Then she creeps to center, lifts a board, reaches down, and extracts a belt, which she straps to herself, then small rectangular packets the size of cigarette packs, which she places in pockets of the belt, and a small unit that resembles a radio, with wires. She looks back at ABE, pulls on her pants, buttons her shirt. He turns, groans.)

(She hovers to assure him, then goes back to extract a revolver and rounds, replace the board, pick up her shoes and her pack, then moves out the door. Morning light, bird sounds. While, outside, she pulls on her shoes, and loads the revolver. Inside, ABE rolls over swiftly and sits up, listening. With revolver in hand, SABRA moves back to the door. ABE hears her coming and lies back down as though asleep. SABRA enters, approaches him quietly, stands over him, with the revolver poised. He is still. Suddenly, as she turns to leave, he rolls, and tackles her. The gun flies out of her hand.)

ABE: Delilah!

SABRA: *(Struggling)* No!

ABE: *(Howls)* Delilah!

SABRA: Let go! You'll get hurt!

ABE: *I'll* get hurt. You thieving bitch! You sneaking, poisonous bitch! Why should I let you go? So you can reach your gun?

(He's pinned her with his weight, now bends her arm. She cries out in pain.)

SABRA: Ahaaah!

ABE: You're a terrorist.

SABRA: No...

ABE: Shut up! You are! And I'm a first rate Jew-guilt sap. What a joke. Hilarious.

SABRA: Abraham...

ABE: Don't talk to me. Don't you *dare* use my name. Bitch!

SABRA: I have to go.

ABE: Sure you do.

SABRA: I have to go before your soldiers come.

ABE: Why didn't you slice my gut open? Why didn't you cut out my heart?

SABRA: Yes! Why didn't I?

ABE: *(Stopped. Realizes)* Because you've got a bigger plan. Not just to butcher me. You've planted a bomb. I saw you, witch!

(ABE *finds he can hobble—with extreme pain, but without passing out.* SABRA's *frightened.*)

ABE: Where?

(She won't respond. He pulls up on her arm. She yells.)

SABRA: Ahaa!

ABE: Where is it?

(She doesn't answer.)

ABE: You figured you'd get us all at once. Where did you put it, bitch!

(He yanks her arm again. She yells, then gasps.)

ABE: You think I won't break it?

SABRA: *(Gasping)* You think I'll tell?

ABE: Of course not. Come on.

(He lurches to the doorway, leaning on her, with her arm locked. She screams with pain.)

SABRA: Abraham, I told you...

ABE: ...lies! Lots of lies. *(Beat)* Here. By the door? So when it shuts we get it in the face? Kaboom! Oh, baby, you should have blown me away when you had the chance. Because you've got another load set to rip my buddy's guts out, and nothing, nothing is a bloody enough way to settle with you!

(He's jerking her around with him, trying to find wires or a telltale sign of a fresh mine planted.)

ABE: Stick with me, cause if it finds us before you give me the word, you're going with me...all the way, baby. *(As he pulls her)* Why the hell did you have to hit on me! What kind of sickness was that? Answer me!! *(Yanking her arm)*

SABRA: Ahhahhh!

(He lets loose, she's gasping, her strength gone, sliding down. ABE, gasping himself, and collapsing from pain, braces himself up off the ground, suddenly realizing—)

ABE: You did it, didn't you. You planted the shit that hit Benny.

(Still breathing hard, she looks at him.)

ABE: Didn't you?!

SABRA: *(Pause. Her eyes on him)* You won't believe me. So believe what you want.

ABE: You bitch...

SABRA: I told you...

ABE: You told me lies!

SABRA: I told you everything I could. You'll understand after...

ABE: After what?!

SABRA: There's nothing to find. You have to let me go.

ABE: I saw you with the stuff!

(He grabs her round the middle, and feels the bulk of her belt just as she swings her leg, ramming hard into his injured foot. He's thrown backwards, howling. She scrambles inside after her fallen gun, and picks up his rifle, covering him with it.)

SABRA: Stay there.

(ABE struggles to his feet, frozen, astonished, staring at her.)

ABE: It's on *you*. I felt it.

SABRA: *(Breathing hard)* Come back inside, Abraham.

ABE: *(Not moving)* The stuff is on you. *You're* the bomb.

SABRA: Come in. Sit down.

ABE: Why. *(Pause. Not moving)* Why?

SABRA: I don't want to hurt you.

ABE: Hah! *(Beat)* What are you doing, Sabra?

SABRA: Nothing that concerns you.

ABE: No?

SABRA: No.

ABE: You're just going to blow yourself up.

SABRA: Maybe.

ABE: Maybe? When do you decide?

SABRA: I don't.

ABE: You don'! You just hop on down to the border and wait for somebody to shoot you? Or watch for a school bus to ram yourself into? Or what!

SABRA: You'd better go in now. Standing out here isn't good for you.

ABE: Sure. Sure.

(He lurches back through door, flings himself onto the seat. She follows, watching him.)

ABE: So what are you going to do with your jackass? Or should I say, your stud.

(She slings the rifle round her back, checks pistol.)

ABE: You lied to me.

SABRA: Some.

ABE: You're Palestinian.

SABRA: I come from Jerusalem.

ABE: My god. Palestinian.

SABRA: *(Quietly)* I'm going home.

ABE: Dressed like that?

(She moves to the radio, picks it up.)

ABE: That's what was wrong with your story of Hamid. I should have picked it up.

SABRA: *(Swift, animal attack)* It makes sense now? What you did to him? Now that you know he was Palestinian?

ABE: *(Icy)* When were you ever in Jerusalem.

(She turns to him, shakes her head, unable to speak.)

ABE: When?!

SABRA: *(Hoarsely)* Never.

ABE: *(Triumphant)* Never.

(She walks close to him, brings her face close to his, and, shaking her head, whispers—)

SABRA: Never.

ABE: *(Understanding, sorry he gloated—)* Sabra...

RADIO: *(V O)* Dogstar to Apex.

(Radio startles SABRA; *then fast, overlapping.)*

SABRA: *(Stepping back)* I know there were oranges there. On the hill. In the night Jew soldiers came, firing shots, shouting loud "Get out!" My father was six. His eyes opened wide—the first time he ever saw soldiers. "Get out, or we'll kill you!"

RADIO: *(V O)* Dogstar to Apex.

SABRA: My grandfather had no gun. "I can't leave my garden, my trees!" My father held his little dove under his shirt.

RADIO: *(V O)* Apex, come in.

SABRA: A soldier took his mother by the hair and dragged her.

RADIO: *(V O)* Are you there? Apex.

*(*SABRA *stares at the radio, hands it to* ABE, *but aims the pistol at him, clicking off safety.)*

SABRA: *(As a soldier, in her story)* "Keep moving."

ABE: Apex here. You're up early. *(Watching* SABRA*)* Is...Benny...

RADIO: *(V O)* Benny hung on. He may make it.

SABRA: "Keep moving..."

ABE: *(Yell)* Benny's alive!

*(*SABRA, *oblivious, can't stop her story—)*

SABRA: "Keep moving!" Guns jabbed my family into the road, where hundreds of families were running, as though from fire.

RADIO: *(V O)* Good news?

SABRA: "Please, let us go back for the stove, for the trunk, for some bread!" There were old who barely could walk, babies clinging to sleeves. "Keep moving!"

RADIO: *(V O)* Apex?

SABRA: The third day his mother stumbled and didn't get up. They dug a hole by the road. The dove was lost before that.

RADIO: *(V O)* Apex? You all right?

ABE: *(Looking at* SABRA*)* Great shape. About to hop in there.

RADIO: *(V O)* Stay where you are. We're on the way.

*(*SABRA *snatches the radio, switches it off.* ABE *still stares at her, then—)*

ABE: That's a story, Sabra.

SABRA: Mine.

ABE: A war story.

SABRA: What war? My family was just living!

ABE: I've got stories, too. Want to hear them? Stories like this are passed down and down...

SABRA: This one you should understand...

ABE: ...and *changed.*

SABRA: ...if your grandmother lost her...

ABE: Don't you dare! My grandmother has nothing to do with you.

SABRA: *(Stepping away, quietly)* "Wait just till the fighting stops." his father said. But when it did, and they started home... The border was shut. With machine guns.

ABE: Just get out of here, why don't you? They're on the way.

SABRA: They took his father for "questioning." The family waited. He didn't return. *(Beat)* I was born in Sabra.

ABE: *(Startled, uneasy)* The camp?

SABRA: The camp. *(Pause)* But my father couldn't forget his father's oranges. He went to fight his way back. When I was eight, Israelis came to Sabra. They surrounded the camp with their tanks. They sent in soldiers...

ABE: *(Sharp)* Not Israeli soldiers!

SABRA: No.

ABE: Not Jews! Arabs.

SABRA: You don't want to hear this story?

ABE: Why don't you kill me? You've come to kill people.

SABRA: Jews.

ABE: People with children.

SABRA: And oranges. People with homes. But who? The Jews who stole my grandfather's orchard, the ones who made Hamid blind, the ones who stood outside the fence while my mother was...

ABE: I'm a Jew. And they aren't me!

SABRA: But you're the only one I know.

ABE: So kill me! *(Pause)* You can't.

SABRA: Yes I can. I kept thinking of ways.

ABE: Does your God enjoy killing?!

SABRA: Does yours?

ABE: *(Almost laughing)* Oh, you'll be welcome in
Jerusalem. Center of the world, city of God, the first
God ever to say "you must not kill." Where everyone
says they come to worship, but what they do there is
hate. The city stinks of blood. *(Pause)* They'll tell you
there's another Jerusalem. A pure one, hanging above
the first one in the sky. It's a lie. There's only one. And
it is brilliant, breathtaking. So why can't its golden light
burn off its poison!

*(He looks at her, exhausted, and as bitter sarcasm surges,
he goes on, fiercely—)*

ABE: Jews aren't as sure as you think, Sabra. With all
you Arabs wanting us dead, we worry we wandered
too many years. We fear it's only you who belong.
So *tell* me!

(She stares at him.)

ABE: About Sabra.

SABRA: *(Choked)* You don't want to know.

ABE: That's right! But I have *no* choice.

*(Frightened by his fierceness, and by approaching the story,
she nearly whispers, fast—)*

SABRA: It wasn't Israelis. You're right. They kept their
hands clean. They only opened the gates.

ABE: *(Hoarse, holding off the experience as long as he can)*
It was Christians, Sabra. It was Christians who went
into Sabra.

*(She looks at him, drawing into herself, and telling a simple
story, with no emotion.)*

SABRA: I'd gone to the edge of the camp for bread.
The babies were crying, hungry again.Angry Timur,
just three, and Somaya, who'd sucked Mama dry. I saw
Israeli tanks lined up by the fence. The firing didn't
scare me much. There was always shooting. I scuttled

from shadow to shadow, past sundown now, curfew already, but I got through. I was skinny as a shadow.

On our alley, soldiers were banging at Aruri's, shouting "open up," and that frightened me. I could hear muffled screams down the alley. A man ran past. A shot flashed beside me. He fell, but I wasn't surprised, only wanting to get home fast. Darting, I came to our door, put my hand in the light flowing out. I was glad it cracked open, but about to scold Mama for not barring it tight, when I heard her moan—a deep terrible sound—then I saw. I saw past the soldier's legs to where little Timur was spread on the floor, opened, like a messy fountain, bubbling bright red.

ABE: No, Sabra, no...

SABRA: My mouth opened, but nothing came out. A hatchet hung from the soldier's fist. Mama was pressed to the wall clutching Somaya, I heard her "I swear, this one's a girl." But he tore the baby from Mama, and grunting, hurled her against the wall. "Girls become mothers. Mothers breed sons." Then he brought down his iron-spiked boot, hard on Somaya's face. I shrieked "Mama!" and jumped for his boot in the air, but he whacked me off with his hatchet, and thumped again with his spike, and again, and again, mashing her tiny face. Then he must have been tired, for he twisted back, and swung his hatchet only once more, slicing my Mama's belly straight through. She bent her head forward without a sound. I crawled to her lap. It was warm a long time.

(Finished, SABRA sits silent. ABE is limp. He wants to help, but hoarsely, all that comes out is—)

ABE: The Lord is my shepherd...

SABRA: *(Softly finishes it—)* ...I shall not want.

ABE: When I asked how Gramma survived, she said that, but... *(Trails off, then—)* Um Sa'ad?

SABRA: Um Sa'ad found me in Mama's lap. I let her
wash me. But I didn't speak...for seven years.

ABE: *(Stares at her. Then, quietly, the last word)* But
life...didn't end.

(SABRA looks at him, her face clears, as though released.)

SABRA: Sa'ad and Hamid were good to me, while they
stayed. But now, Um Sa'ad only rocks on her stoop and
talks about olives. She doesn't remember this dead life.
She only dreams of home.

ABE: Sabra... Stay with me.

SABRA: *(Beat)* A lost home is a kind of disease, you
know. It drains off your soul.

ABE: I know.

SABRA: Some people leave their homes. Or deny them.
But they're never lost.

ABE: No.

SABRA: *(Beginning to feel life)* So I promised her I'd go,
I'd find it. And if I get to Jerusalem, the others can come.

ABE: You'll die, Sabra. How far can you get?

SABRA: *(Clear, happy)* I can't tell. The land will know me.
When I touch it...I'll be alive. And the joy...! *(She breaks
off, imagining the moment.)*

ABE: You're going to kill people.

SABRA: I won't if they let me pass. I'll warn them.

ABE: If you warn them, they'll shoot you. You'll
explode alone.

SABRA: But they'll know it's my home. Why else would
I die just to get there?

(He stares at her.)

ABE: You're insane.

SABRA: Am I? *Think.* If you were me? What would you do.

(He looks at her without an answer. SABRA takes the radio, begins to move out.)

ABE: If you take my rifle...

SABRA: If I leave it, you'll shoot me.

(He turns away sharply, and she's sorry for saying it.)

SABRA: You'd have to shoot me. Do you want the choice?

ABE: *(Beat)* I'll be naked out here. Your "brothers" will be happy to find me.

SABRA: I'll leave it a hundred yards out, against a tree. You can make it that far.

ABE: But the radio. If they call me again...

SABRA: You'll tell them.

ABE: No, you'll be safer if...

SABRA: You'll call and tell them.

ABE: If they can't reach me, they'll know something's wrong.

SABRA: They'll come just as fast either way.

ABE: But they'll bring more men.

SABRA: Shut up! You can't stop me!

ABE: That's right!

(SABRA moves quickly to door. ABE throws himself to stop her—)

ABE: Oh, Sabra, my love... *(But his foot folds under him, he falls to the ground)* ...my little one, wait. Just wait. I'll think of something. Please..

SABRA: Abraham...

ABE: *(Suddenly clear)* I'll take you to Jerusalem.

(She stares at him, astonished an instant, then shouts.)

SABRA: Don't say that!

(She sobs uncontrollably, he lurches toward her, pulling her to her knees, with him.)

ABE: Yes, yes, please, listen my love.

(He embraces her, ignoring the weapons and radio.)

ABE: Don't cry, it's over now. That's what we'll do. I'll take you there. We'll go together.

SABRA: *(Clear, quiet)* You can't.

ABE: Why not?

SABRA: You know you can't.

ABE: What can't I do? If I love you, I can do anything.

SABRA: *(Staring at him, calm, backing away)* You're speaking like a child.

ABE: Maybe. Maybe it needs a child. Then that's what I'll be. Let me take you. We'll find the tree together, the old wall, the eggplants.

SABRA: *(Gutteral, pained)* Abraham...

ABE: That's how it should be. I know the way.

SABRA: Please...

ABE: The air is so light there. It chimes. On the hillside, we could sing, we could make a child...

SABRA: You're talking magic. Don't! It's not fair!

ABE: Magic does happen. Do you believe I love you?

SABRA: *(Carefully—)* In this moment...yes.

ABE: Then, in this moment, I can do whatever it takes.

SABRA: What can you do.

ABE: I don't know. We have to think, we have to plan.

(He holds her, and she him.)

ABE: Oh my love. *(Takes her by the shoulders)* The first thing is... We have to... *(Embarrassed laugh)*...unhook you. I can't hold onto a fully-armed bomb.

SABRA: *(Backing away, wary)* The connection isn't live. I didn't hook it yet.

ABE: Let me see at least, Sabra.

(Still staying away from him, she lifts her shirt, revealing the belt, the packs in place, and the ignition pack in the center of her belly. He inhales sharply, nearly unnerved.)

ABE: Let's take it off, please.

SABRA: Not yet.

ABE: You don't believe me.

SABRA: I don't know if you can do what you say.

ABE: But you want me to.

SABRA: It's a dream.

ABE: You're awake, Sabra. We both are.

SABRA: How could we go there?

ABE: First, it has to seem natural. We'll say you're Lebanese, and I met you before I...

SABRA: No! They can't see me! I won't. They'll lock me up.

ABE: Why? Did you do something else?

SABRA: No, Abraham. I don't have to "do something" to get locked up. Hamid didn't "do something."

ABE: But we can tell them...

SABRA: No! It's impossible. They'll never let me in.

(The radio crackles, in her hand. They stare at each other.)

RADIO: *(V O)* Dogstar to Apex. Dogstar to Apex.

(She twists, about to run, but he grabs her)

ABE: I'm going to marry you, Sabra.

(Stopped, she looks at him, hands him the radio, and backs off. While she watches him, and he her, she hooks up the wires on her belt. Controlling his alarm, ABE speaks into the radio.)

ABE: Apex here. What's for breakfast?

RADIO: *(V O)* We're five clicks and counting. Gear up.

ABE: Roger. *(He lowers the radio, and spreads his arms.)* You can kill me now. They'll never know what happened.

(She looks at him, then runs to embrace him.)

ABE: Careful. Careful with you. I'm not going to let you go, not going to let anyone hurt you. Do you understand me?

SABRA: Yes.

ABE: If you won't face them, then you'll have to hide here. We'll have to meet later.

SABRA: You can't come here alone. And even if you could, then what? There's no way to "take" me there.

ABE: Can you get to Tyre?

SABRA: I can get anywhere.

ABE: I don't like it. There's too much chance to lose you.

SABRA: I know.

ABE: I'll get you papers. A passport.

SABRA: *(Gasps, overjoyed)* A passport?! A real pass...

ABE: You know it...

(He hesitates, she finishes the thought.)

SABRA: ...couldn't say Palestinian.

ABE: It would have to say...

SABRA: *(Interrupting)* It's no good, Abraham.
You'd ruin your life.

ABE: *My* life?

SABRA: You'd be a traitor. Someone would know.
And any Israeli would do anything to stop you,
anything. Terrible things would happen, against
your will. And they'd never let me live.

ABE: *(Amused at her)* Israelis aren't as bad as you believe.

SABRA: It can't work. As soon as I do something,
anything you don't like, you'll turn on me.
You'd never trust me.

ABE: Stop insulting me!

SABRA: There's no time, Abraham. They're getting close.
Just let me hide. I've come this far.

ABE: *(Frustrated, it bursts out)* I can't leave you loose
here!

SABRA: That's it. I might betray you. Well, maybe you'll
have to shoot me.

(She offers him his rifle, and her revolver.)

SABRA: If I give you this? Will you still be afraid I'll hurt
someone?

ABE: *(Taking the rifle, roughly)* Besides you, you mean?

SABRA: So it's your duty to shoot me. *(Pause, waiting for
him to do it)* You better not tell them anything about us.
They'll think you went mad.

(She abruptly moves to leave. He lunges for her.)

ABE: Stop it!

SABRA: Be careful, I'm live!

ABE: Stop wasting the time! I'm not letting you go.
I'm going to take you to Jerusalem, even if we have
to cross the border under machine guns! So stop this.
You've got to trust me!

SABRA: *(Anguished)* There is no way, Abraham.

ABE: *(In a rush, tight—)* All you've known is a
nightmare. But I'm strong. I have my home. My only
nightmare is fighting your fear. My strength is enough
for us both. You have to believe in me, now, believe we
have hope.

(She's quiet. He kisses her.)

ABE: I'm going to find out where they are. *(Calls on the
radio, holding her, looking at her)* Apex to Dogstar.

RADIO: *(V O)* Dogstar to Apex. Afraid we'll sneak up on
you?

ABE: Where are you?

RADIO: *(V O)* Just passing Beaufort Castle. You'll hear
us any minute. All clear?

ABE: Everything's quiet. Thanks. *(Clicks off radio,
holds her quietly, speaks clearly)* Get me a sealed message.
Bring it to I D F Central in Tyre. Give it to my friend,
Eli. He's at the gate every day from eight to four.

*(She's fastened on him hopefully. Getting an idea, he grins at
her.)*

ABE: My boot! Extra dogtags.

SABRA: What?

(He's pulling out the dogtags she found.)

ABE: Here's who you want to find. But I'm keeping half
of it.

(He breaks it in two, and hands her the half on the string.)

ABE: Half stays with the body, half goes...elsewhere.

SABRA: *(Holds him tight)* Oh, Abraham.

ABE: In the message, just tell me where you'll be next Saturday, all day. I'll get leave and a ride there. Anywhere you say. Do you believe me?

SABRA: Yes.

ABE: Unhook this now.

(She looks at him, uncertain.)

ABE: Please. I won't ask you to take it off. Only... to take care of my love.

(She carefully disarms the ignition pack.)

ABE: Now answer me something.

SABRA: *(Smiles)* What can I answer you?

ABE: If you hadn't planned to die today...would you have made love to me last night?

SABRA: *(Sober)* Of course not!

(He laughs, holding her, rocking her.)

ABE: I don't even know how to feel about that. Sabra... Sabra...

SABRA: How will you take me to Jerusalem, Abraham?

ABE: As my wife. Don't you see? You can be anyone.

SABRA: Even an Israeli wife.

ABE: Even that.

SABRA: But not Palestinian.

ABE: Sabra, Sabra...no one can make you anyone but who you are.

SABRA: But if I pretend, I can be happy. *(Beat)* What about Um Sa'ad. *(Then, calmly, knowing—)* It's no good, is it. If I don't touch the land on my own, I haven't done anything. I've abandoned them all.

ABE: No you haven't. Not if you're happy.

SABRA: That's your love speaking.

ABE: Yes!

SABRA: *(Smiling, kisses him)* You're so strong.
My invincible enemy. And I can rest, you'll always
protect me...because you love me.

ABE: Yes.

SABRA: *(Gently pulling away from him)* Then you'll
understand.

*(Noise off, soldiers moving. SABRA hears, goes to draw aside
the rope that revealed the cave.)*

ABE: *(A reflex, not understanding)* Don't go...

SABRA: I have to, Abraham. Please forgive me.

*(SABRA moves outside, and as ABE stumbles after her,
cave ropes lift.)*

ABE: What? You have to stay here.

*(SABRA is moving, increasing the space between them,
through center stage that was the cave.)*

SABRA: Um Sa'ad needs her joy back. Listen my love.
If I live and get there, she'll know she exists.

ABE: It's too late to go!

*(ABE and SABRA are in opposite corners where each first
appeared.)*

SABRA: I'll be all right. I'll go quickly; I'll make it,
don't worry.

ABE: You can't!

SABRA: I won't forget you, Abraham. I married you here.

(Then she runs away, disappears, as—)

ABE: Wait. You can't go. You can't go! It's too late to go. Come back, Sabra. Come back!

DOG-STAR: *(Muffled, Off)* Abe, are you there?

ABE: I'll keep you safe. I'll take you to Jerusalem!

DOG-STAR: *(Off)* Advise, Abe?! What's going on?

ABE: Don't leave me here!!

DOG-STAR: *(Alarmed, off)* Abe, where are you? Halt!

ABE: No!

DOG-STAR: *(Off)* Halt, or I'll shoot!

ABE: *(Scream)* Don't shoot, don't shoot!!

(Shots off. Then an explosion from the direction SABRA ran. ABE drops to his knees, arms spread.)

ABE: Sabra.

(As lights fade to only the glow of the explosion and a spot on ABE's face, GRAMMA speaks, over-laid with Hebrew and Arabic, blending in music.)

GRAMMA: *(V O, almost a whisper)* Surely goodness and mercy will follow me all the days of my life, and I will dwell in the house of the Lord forever.

(Blackout)

END OF PLAY

www.ingramcontent.com/pod-product-compliance
Lightning Source LLC
Chambersburg PA
CBHW052221090426
42741CB00010B/2623